HOW TO TELL YOUR KID...

(THE 10 WORST DAYS OF MY LIFE)

CAITLIN CONGDON

How To Tell your Kid
The 10 worst days of my life

Published by Spines
ISBN: 979-8-89383-209-9

ACKNOWLEDGMENTS

This book is in loving memory of my mother....

Bronwyn "Anne" Congdon

1965-2024

1

I come from a very big family. I am one of 5 siblings, three girls and two boys. My oldest sister has six children. I have one son. And my little brother, 3rd in the line-up, has one daughter. My mother was adopted at birth, and so was her brother, my uncle Kenyon. Other than my grandmother (Mary Fickett), my family has never really experienced death....let alone spoken about it. We never really had any serious talks about anything...death, sex...nothing.

2

As I become older, I start to realize you can't escape any of it. You HAVE to / NEED to talk about it. And now that I have a son of my own, I wish I had been told what to say, what to do, or how to act when the world caves in on itself.....

3

———

My family, except for a slight few, are not very religious. I was raised to know/believe there is a higher power but not to know exactly what that is. I was never truly told where we go in our next life. Or what exactly awaits us.... I think we all just kinda took what we were told and made it our own..

So when my world started to crumble, I had no idea what to do, and I did the best I could.

4

January 11 2024

It started with the passing of a very good friend of mine, Henry; He had actually just met my whole family just a few months before. He had accompanied me to my sister's wedding that past September. He had known my son since June of that year. He was such a bright and lively soul. He also had three boys, all close to my son's age. We had had a few play dates in the past, and our children enjoyed each other's company.

5

I found out about his passing through social media. I had received a message from his girlfriend a week prior, but because we were not "friends," the notification didn't "ding" when she sent the message. The moment I read it, I knew something was not right.

When I got confirmation of my inner thoughts, and I knew he was gone, I instantly called my best friend, Yelling, " Henry is dead." I didn't know how to act or what to do. I broke down. Screaming, crying, and yelling.

7

———

That was when I noticed my son sitting on the couch. He was insanely upset. He was crying and yelling and asking me what I had said..."Was Henry dead? Tears ran from his eyes, and he ran into his bedroom. That was when I knew I DID NOT handle this well. I went and pulled my son from his room, asking him to sit with me on the couch. Wanting to talk. He was still very upset...panting, crying, and somewhat hesitant.

8

———

I was sorry he had to hear it in that way. I told him he was allowed to feel however he wanted. If he wanted to cry, he could, but he didn't have to. If he wanted to talk, we could do that too.

9

At that moment, my son stopped crying, wiped his tears from his eyes, and grabbed the remote to watch the TV. He continued to turn on one of his favorite shows. He watched it for about 4 minutes and then went back to his room, this time to play with toys.

10

I then realized I needed to fix whatever I had just done. So I waited about 2 hours, and I asked my son to come with me and take a walk in the woods to collect firewood. It was an afternoon in January, so we put on our jackets and headed out.

11

———

I find the outdoors to be very peaceful, and again...I didn't know what I was doing; I was just trying my best to make the situation as calming as possible. So once we were out there for about 20 minutes or so, I asked my 6-year-old son , "Do you know what it means to die?"

My son responded, "They are gone forever, and we will never see them again."

12

I told my child he was right and wrong.

I explained to him that, yes, when people die, they are gone...but I asked, "Do you know where they go?"

He said, "No".

I told him they go to heaven, and they become angels, and the angels are the clouds. So you might not be able to see them the way they were before, but you CAN always see them. All you have to do is look up... so of course, my son looked up. And there was not ONE SINGLE cloud in the sky.

13

———

That, of course, led to more questions...."Mom, why are there no clouds...so where are the angels?"

Off the top of my head.... I responded...."Well, of course, you don't see any clouds; all the angels are having a party welcoming Henry."

My child then looked at me with the brightest look and all the confidence in the world and said, "I hope when I die, Henry will be there with all the angels having a party for me."

14

———————

That was when I knew I had done a good job and had said something right. I didn't make it scary. I didn't make it so deep of a conversation that he had more and more questions. I had explained it at his level.

Very proud of myself but also petrified at his last statement...I responded, "I don't ever wanna hear you say that again. That is a wonderful thought, but you don't need to think about dying anytime soon."

15

January 20 2024

I was at work, and I got a phone call from my dad. He tells me to go somewhere quiet, and he asks me if I am sitting down. Once he gets all his confirmations, he tells me my mother is gone....

My mother had suddenly passed away peacefully in her sleep, at the age of 58. No warning. No time to prepare. No rhyme or reason.

I now had another death. The biggest death. The death that could kill me.

She was the mom of all moms, the mom to more than just her own. The amazing woman who had taught me all I know. Shaped me. And now she was gone???

After a full mental breakdown in the company stairwell and about 10-15 minutes of grasping for air and asking myself if it was real.... a friend drove me home.

So, like I said earlier, I have two brothers and two sisters. And, not tooting my own horn, I know I am labeled as the strong one. I know I have to be able to keep it somewhat together for my siblings. I know I need to be the rock along with my dad. Our family needs us.

17

———

I couldn't be the one to reach out to them. My dad had expressed that he wanted to do it... so I waited.

I was specifically waiting for my oldest sister's phone call. I knew my brothers had their circle of comfort. My youngest sister still lived with my parents,so at the moment, I knew she was with my dad. But my oldest sister.....my mom was the person on this planet. They look the same. Their voice sounded the same.......so I waited for her, but she never called.

18

Instead, it was my oldest niece, my oldest sister's oldest daughter (Haylie). My sister was NOT doing well, and my niece didn't know what to do for her mother. I did the best I could, talking and sometimes yelling at my sister at the moment. Trying to get her to pull it together for her kids. But it all fell on deaf ears: too much emotion, too much sadness, too many tears.

19

My nephew Liam is 12 and slightly autistic. My mother (his grandmother) was his best friend. He had been living with her and my dad for years so he could attend a certain private school. Liam and my mom were two peas in a pod. With my mother passing and my sister (his mom) so emotional, my niece had to tell her brother what was going on, that his grandmother/ his best friend had died.

20

That led to another phone call coming my way....Haylie wanted me to talk to Liam. Again, no one in our family has had to deal with this, and Haylie had done the most she could do. So I explained to Liam that his Momo was not gone. She is just in a different form....She is in the clouds. She is always with us. And you can always see her when you want just by looking up.

By the time we got off the phone, Liam seemed to be doing better. Of course, I explained I was here if he needed me. I knew I could NEVER replace Momo, but I could/would be his best friend..... and I would also be at his house within the hour.

21

———

Once again, I took a deep breath..... I still hadn't even told my own son and hadn't even picked him up from daycare. My world was crumbling, shattering, crashing. And I was dead on the inside.... exhausted from the overwhelming news

I headed to pick up my son. I was so afraid to tell him the news. Especially so close to Henry's passing.

How would he take it? What would he say? What would he ask?Oddly enough, when I told my son about his Momo passing away....he smiled. He asked me if she was with Henry in the clouds.....and he told me they must be having a party.

"Yes, she is. And yes, they are," was my response.

23

That was the first time I had smiled since getting the news of my mother.

Once I arrived at my sister's house, I was informed that no one had told my youngest niece and nephew (2 and 4 years old) what was going on. When I asked why...they told me they were waiting for me....

(The amount of pressure I felt at that moment is almost indescribable. ME! ME! I can NOT mess this up. I can't scare them; I can't be too morbid.)

24

I went to my 4-year-old nephew and picked him up. I sat him on a dresser so we could be eye to eye. I wanted to make sure we were on an even level.... I then explained to him Momo had passed away.... I had to clarify she was dead. It was awful. I also explained to him he could feel however he wanted. He didn't have to cry, but if he wanted to, he could. He didn't have to be sad. I then explained to him that when going home to Momo and Paw-paw's house, he would see a lot of people crying. Everyone was sad and upset. But again, don't cry just because everyone else is, only if you want to. But give hugs. Whenever he saw someone upset, his job was to give hugs and give love.

25

———————

I then went and found my two-year-old niece. I gave her a very similar talk. And wouldn't you know......that's just what they did. They gave hugs and love anytime and every time they saw someone/ anyone upset. They truly helped with the whole process.

Now, I am not a religious person. I wasn't raised to necessarily be one. But I do believe whether it is good or bad. Everything happens for a reason. And yes, I truly loved my Great friend Henry, But I believe I went through his passing, so I could be there for my family in the passing of my mom.

Bronwyn Anne Congdon (1965-2024) was the most amazing mother, wife, and friend. This life of mine and this world will never be the same without her.

If the worst days of my life could help any family or any parents with one of the most difficult conversations, then all of this would be worth it.

AFTERWORD

To all the loved ones, all the memories, and all the families dealing with losing a loved one..... My thoughts and good vibes are with you.

Best Wishes, Caitlin Congdon